√10|03

Memories of Denmead

by

Bessie Blanchard

DEDICATION

*"I dedicate this book to all the villagers of Denmead,
past and present, who have helped to fill
my life with so many memories."*

Bessie Blanchard

Memories of Denmead

Published in 2002 by
Denmead Village Association
Web site: www.denmeadva.f9.co.uk

ISBN 0-9537959-1-8

Printed by Studio 6, The Square, Wickham, Hampshire PO17 5JN
Telephone: 01329-832933 • www.studio-6.co.uk

FORMER PUBLICATIONS

Denmead Papers:

1. Mr John Baggs
2. Denmead Village Association - 'The First 25 Years'
3. 'Growing-up in Denmead - 1920-1950'

Special Millennium Edition 'Journeys to Yesterday' by Terry Norman (Reprint)

CONTENTS

Front cover: Children and mums from Brooklyn Terrace, 1943, collecting salvage for the War effort

ACKNOWLEDGEMENTS

Hampshire - The County Magazine (1985)

DVA Local History Group

Mrs Vivien Chiswell - photographs and typing

Mr Lindsey Maguire of Studio 6 - for his encouragement,
enthusiasm and helpful ideas

.

DISCLAIMER

Please note that all views in this book are personal to Bessie Blanchard.

INTRODUCTION

Denmead Village Association was formed in 1973 to consider the implications of the South Hampshire Structure Plan and its effect on Denmead.

The threat of massive development alarmed the people who wished to keep Denmead separate from Waterlooville and to retain its village identity.

In 1977 the Association was instrumental in achieving phased controlled planning for fifteen years and since then has been prominent in many ways, and still keeps a lively interest in all village affairs. (Denmead Papers II - 'The First 25 Years' explains this fully).

As the village continues to grow it is difficult to hold on to the essence of village life. Many newcomers wish to know more about the history of Denmead, so Denmead Village Association is gathering together the reminiscences of older Denmeadians to this end.

Bessie Blanchard is a well-known much-loved person who over the years has written a number of essays about her life in Denmead which encapsulate the past.

They are unique and as part of the Association's celebration of HM Queen Elizabeth II's Golden Jubilee, they have been collected and published in book form for the people of Denmead to keep and enjoy.

There is some overlapping of details but this is inevitable for these are Bessie's personal reminiscences.

It is hoped that this special edition will evoke memories for older people and provide younger and newer Denmeadians with a deeper insight into village life.

May they be encouraged to 'take part' and keep the community spirit of our village alive.

Edra Goodman

Chairman DVA
January 2002

A LIFETIME IN
Denmead

The Village Pond, 1910

Bessie: "There's a Health Centre there now."

Friend: "How do you mean, a Health Centre? Where did they build that, then?"

"You know, where the village pond was."

"But they can't build a Health Centre on a village pond, can they?"

"Well, they filled the pond in first and then left it alone for ages, then the Health Centre materialised. It certainly looked a most unusual building, but I guess it is a most needed thing even in a village, and who needs a pond these days!"

"Well I never! I remember that old pond by the side of Hambledon Road, it had a white posted iron bar fence along by the side of the road, didn't it?"

"Yes, and at the back, a big willow tree was overhanging where the ducks used to nest under its branches. That was a dirty old pond though! How many children in their time fell in the water, on their way home from school? And what about trying

The Health Centre

the ice on a cold winter's day, and watching the ice crack? Yes, and their mums couldn't get their clothes dry to wear to school the next morning."

"Mind you, we walked to school in those days. I only had one mile to walk each day, but my friends who lived up at Eastland Gate or World's End or Pit Hill of course had much further, about three miles each way. Sometimes I've known them to cut through the fields on the footpaths to their homes, but come rain or snow they never stayed away from school. Do you remember our Headmaster then?"

"Yes, of course I do, it was Dave Cleary, wasn't it?"

"Well, yes, but before him, when I started school, it was Mr Harry Cross. He left suddenly, went away from the village, so then we had a Headmistress. She wasn't liked very much because her surname happened to be Miss Whipp!"

"The School Beadle, as we used to call him, was Mr Strickland. We didn't dare stay at home in those days or else we were in front of the class next morning and in disgrace with the teachers, unless we were really ill, then all would be forgiven. Hambledon village had an outbreak of diphtheria, and my friend died with it, she was only ten years old. Because Hambledon had it so bad, Denmead School every morning lined the children up in each classroom and each child had to gargle with Conde's Fluid. Thankfully the epidemic subsided and diphtheria never seemed to be as bad again in the years ahead."

The school had a very good building, boasting two playgrounds, one for boys and one for girls, with the big garden belonging to the Headmaster's house separating the two playgrounds. We used to tend his garden, the boys digging it and the girls used to pick the fruit and pickle the onions. All good for the life of a country child, I suppose.

There were a lot of children attending the school before the War; the surrounding villages were growing and so we had intakes from Purbrook, Cowplain and other places. Being just a village child living in Denmead, it did one good to broaden one's outlook by mixing with other outsiders. During those years at school we had a great happening which many a person who lived in Denmead then will remember very clearly. It was the sudden death of Vicar Green. He had been Vicar for 50 years and was nearing 80 when he passed away, sadly mourned by all the villagers, most of all by the children. On the day of the funeral the children walked in twos to the church with the Head Boy and Girl carrying a very large white cross.

I don't remember much else till we arrived at the graveside and as the children filed past they each threw a flower in the moss-lined grave. He was a very popular man. He used to visit the school each week and as soon as he opened the teacher's gate off the Hambledon Road the children would swarm around just to hold his hand

and touch his coat. He was such a very loving man to the children of the village and his word was law. In fact if any boys were to be punished for wrongs they had done they had to report to Vicar Green and they would abide by his decision. Vicar Green had planted fir trees round the school playground and on the side of the pathway going to the churchyard and round the cemetery. I believe it's been said he always had seed in his pocket. Now those trees are mostly gone, but there are a few left as a reminder.

Ashling House - built 1810

The lovely mansion house 'Ashling House', was on the Southwick Road. There was a farm on the corner belonging to it. A lovely flint wall had broken glass on the top to stop people from climbing over, I suppose, although many a lad would climb the walls just for fun. The house used to be owned by the Tayler family, great church people, who did a tremendous lot for the community. Lovely fêtes were held in their grounds. Dancing and even gymkhanas were held each year and all the lawns were lit up with fairy lights during the evening. During the War the house and grounds became occupied by the Army, it was their HQ.

They also took over other places, one place known as the Craigstone Club, a club formed years ago belonging to a Captain Marriot, a Naval officer: I believe it's still a very popular place to go (now The Mead End).

During the Coronation night of King George VI and Queen Elizabeth in 1937, the whole village was invited to Craigstone to celebrate there as a free gesture, but during the evening it was raided by police, and many were fined; even many church people celebrated there quite innocently but the village lived it down, although a report was in the newspapers. Bessie was there and so was Reverend Miller - he only drank lemonade. His picture was in the Evening News which may have prompted a visit from the Archdeacon a few days later when Bessie was scrubbing the Vicarage steps. In Mead End Road in the fields opposite where a housing estate has now been built, was a gun park. They also made a nice cement road near Ashling House which now is Ashling Park Road. So even the Army brought a lot of good to the village. Many a soldier married a local girl and even today they come back to the village to visit.

Beautiful trees surrounded the Ashling estate. As a child I would go with others and collect up acorns; during the War the farmers would pay us 6d a sandbag-full as feed for the pigs, so then we had a bit of pocket money. We also ran messages for our neighbours, mostly delivering washing which was done by most housewives being at home all day, and we got a little gift like a cake or an apple and sometimes pennies if we were lucky. Sometimes the people were too poor and even the washing was done free by the neighbours to help a family.

There was a sweet shop where we used to spend our halfpennies, just up the hill from the school, called Miss McGee's; it was a conservatory attached to the house and we used to love to run up there in our dinner time and just gaze at the grand display of all kinds of sweets. Then the shop closed and another shop was built on the opposite side of the road and Miss McGee no longer sold sweets. The other shop was owned by Mr Cox who stayed for many years, but of course I left school then and didn't visit up there much after that. A field nearby on Mr Green's farm used to be full of cowslips and as a child I have picked many a bunch and then walked back through the woods and allotments to home where many an elderly person would welcome a bunch in those days.

Talking about allotments, we had lovely Sunday walks during the summer with our relations from away. We used to walk down Kidmore Lane; we didn't call it Kidmore in those days, it was commonly called Stares' Lane after the farm halfway along; Mr Stares owned Pyles Farm.

Pyles Farm

We would walk through the path to the churchyard and there were little fir trees planted all round it and alongside the path, and there used to be four trees right in the centre of the churchyard cemetery where Vicar Green intended to be buried, but sorry to say, the trees grew too close to each other and his grave is now on the side not far from where the trees were, although all the trees have been cut down. Didn't the place look very bare afterwards! We often used to see Reverend Green at his garden gate along the churchyard path.

Getting back to our Sunday walk, we would go over the stile to Fairholme field, which had a right of way diagonally across from the stile at churchyard path to a stile at the allotments. Then we would go down the side picking our way carefully by the garden of Fairholme where masses of snowdrops would grow, on into the lower allotments and into the woods which used to be full of primroses and bluebells. There was, and still is today, a big dell there; I think it's where the flint stones were taken for building the walls and houses in the village. It was a lovely walk, one never got tired of it.

There were strawberry teas each year at Stares' Farm, and we would eat as many as we liked with loads of cream, and the games we could play afterwards round the farm! It was to celebrate the birthday of Mrs Stares and her twin sister; of course we had to pay, only sixpence though, and it was always a lovely day out each year.

There were some interesting walks we would take and it was simple to cut through a field, go into a dell and spend the day there picking flowers, bird nesting, climbing trees and sliding down the banks on a piece of galvanised sheeting, or just sliding down. We used to be pretty tired by the time we got home, and the flowers had all gone to sleep, so had to be bunched and put in jam jars of water and left on the windowsills outside all night with probably a jar of tadpoles. There used to be a group of beech trees at the crossroads before Pit Hill, where we used to carve our initials on the trunks, but time has gone by and now no lovely beech trees stand, and a lot of the dells no longer exist.

There were cottages at the bottom of Pit Hill, I believe one was a blacksmith's cottage. Each cottage had apple trees with their branches hanging over the lanes, where a person could reach up and pick them, and in a field at the bottom, mushrooms grew in their hundreds, it used to be white with them. Now we only seem to buy cultivated ones, don't we?

There was plenty to occupy one living in Denmead. On our way home from a walk there were always the families at the cottage garden gates leaning over to talk to anyone passing by, so it often got dark by the time we left them. Then we would get a bit worried as we could see the lights going up on Portsdown Hill - about four in those days, although now it's one big illumination. I believe the four lights were for aircraft guidance at the time.

There were a good few shops in Denmead at one time. We had one at the Forest of Bere, a general shop, and another one opposite, both have been demolished. I remember round Furzely Corner on our way to Purbrook we could get sweets to buy from a little shop attached to a house, which was just a front room, but we enjoyed buying sweets there while out walking during the hot weather, usually pushing children in a pram. Sometimes we would walk to Sheepwash Farm. There was a stream with a tunnel under the road where children could run through. We would fish for minnows there, and the water was lovely and clean, so interesting that we usually came away with our shoes all wet and muddy and a long way to walk home.

At Eastland Gate, going towards Lovedean, there was another shop; on the corner at the Eastland Gate crossroad there was a farm and house called The Arrows. This was a general shop and bakery. There is just a nice house there now, as I suppose a shop wouldn't do much trade in these days.

It was quite safe walking round the lanes. If we ever met any traffic it would probably be a horse and cart or a bicycle. Cars were few and far between. Then as they came by, we would get ourselves into the hedge as the lanes were very narrow and not made up. There was usually a cart track in most lanes. If it rained while we were out we would stop and take shelter in a barn or under a tree until the worst of the rain passed over as we never wore macs; most people had a big overcoat, thick and heavy, and a hat, so the clothes took a couple of days to dry before they could be worn again. Most families in Denmead only had a range fire to do everything by, and usually a line going across the room to air the clothes. One could always go wooding and so we never really went cold even during the War, when coal was rationed.

I remember often coming home from school about 4 p.m.; we used to take a can, and walk up to Stares' Farm, to buy separated milk, which was used for making milk puddings the following day and the milk being separated was a lot cheaper. There used to be quite a few children getting the milk, and on the way back home we used to play about and swing the milk over our heads. Needless to say, the milk got spilt and back to the farm we would go, and usually the farmer's wife would let us have another lot, but would caution us very severely for wasting it.

We had a milkman who called each day; he had a lovely horse and cart: a yellow cart with a big churn at the back with a tap attached to it and a special pail with a lid and measure. The housewife would come to the door with her jug to be filled. He always gave extra measure, not just a pint like we have today in bottles, but the sad part was if it was a very cold morning, the jug might slip out of the milkman's hands and break, so jugs were very scarce in those days, and much in demand. When we were very small the milkman would allow us children a little ride on the back of the cart as the horse was so quiet and well trained, and never went very fast.

Another vehicle we used to ride on was a motor truck belonging to Mr May the Carrier from Hambledon. He had an old lorry with the tailboard down at the back. As children we could climb up and sit at the back while he was going along the road.

He called at different houses on the way to Portsmouth each week and delivered parcels and different items. He would call at a person's house, charge five pence for delivery of, perhaps, a joint of meat or fresh fish which he used to buy at Charlotte Street market, or perhaps collect a piece of furniture or a bicycle from the station. He often had a sack of ice on the back of his truck (for a tradesman, I suppose) and when we children sat at the back the ice used to make us wet where we had been sitting on it.

If we wanted any haberdashery, woollens or knitting wools or painting books, etc., we would go to a shop at the end of Brooklyn Terrace belonging to Mr Gould. His daughter Grace served behind the counter for most of her life. She was a cripple and was unable to walk about, so all the goods were always near to hand, usually wrapped up in brown paper or in closed boxes and one would have to wait until she opened them up, for the customer couldn't handle them till they were paid for. I remember the bell over the door, as one turned the handle to go in the shop, and on the floor was brown paper drawing-pinned down so the dirt from one's shoes didn't tread onto the lino. It was great excitement to go in the shop just to buy ribbon or some little thing when we had only a penny to spend. And Miss Gould sold lovely magic painting books which kept a child quiet for many an hour in the winter.

The Chapel is now the Baptist Church. As children we used to love to go to Sunday School there. There were outings to Hayling every year and the Christmas parties were held in the back room of the Chapel.

Baptist Church, Anmore Road

I remember the field next to the Chapel where we used to play. It was always known as Tee's field, a lovely small field, ideal for children, especially for the Terrace children in Anmore Road. We used to run through the alleyways across the road and over the ditch and up the back and into the field summer or winter; imagine trying to do that now with the traffic travelling along the road at 50mph! It's a blessing now to know that the field has been built on and some lovely bungalows are there. The oak trees at the back are still standing. The lads used to climb trees and swing from branch to branch and cross over to each tree.

They often fell with bruises and torn trousers, and nearly every boy had patches on the seat of his trousers in those days!

Many a family from the Terrace would sit out in the field in the summer to have photographs taken with perhaps the Chapel in the background. During the War soldiers had a camp there with a big kitchen going for the D-Day troops passing by. Anmore Road was full of Army vehicles for weeks parked along by the Terrace. One night in an air raid an incendiary bomb set light to a truck and as there was so much ammunition around the Army pushed the vehicle up the road away from the houses, thus saving our Terrace.

Another big field at the back of Tee's field was known as the Forest, and the pond there had bulrushes, lovely brown-headed ones; we used to gather them for a vase by the fireplace. We loved to catch lizards and frogs and snakes there. I think the pond has been filled in now. We children would acquire a long bean stick, tie a piece of string on it, attach a safety pin with a worm on the end, oh yes, and a matchstick for a float and fish for the lizards; they were lovely colours.

We spent hours playing in those fields and at haymaking time we were allowed in the Forest to play with the hay as it would dry quicker if we tossed it about. Going down the bottom of the Forest onto the lane there used to be the hayrick. There was a horse going round and round all day driving the elevator to carry the hay up to the top of the rick. There was always a crowd standing round watching the machine, usually a dog or two ready to catch the mice. My brother would come home with them in his pocket, put them in one pocket and they would nibble their way through to the other pocket, the coat being lined throughout.

That all caused plenty of excitement in those days. Of course there was another playing field down Edney's Lane called the Peak where most of the football matches were played and now a large playing field has been made where the grounds of Ashling House were.

In the past we lived in Denmead as one big family; one would know everybody by name and so we all grew up together. We only had two schools in those days. There was Miss Buchanan's Collegiate School, where children paid to be educated. It started off in a room of a house opposite the Memorial Hall, then as the village grew and more children attended so Miss Buchanan moved on the opposite side of the Hambledon Road. Miss Buchanan specialised in music and French, so there was a great team spirit which still stands today between those who attended her school and others who attended the Council School. It's a way of life, I suppose, like Oxford and Cambridge.

Many children educated at either school have made very good progress ending up with their own businesses. We never had the trouble with hooliganism, it soon got knocked out of children if they made trouble.

We had our village Policeman on patrol walking, or usually on a bicycle. He used to live at Brooklyn Terrace but later moved opposite the Anthill Common School. Then later a special policeman's house was built at Park Road, where of course it is more central.

Restall's shop still stands, but with many different changes in the years. At one time there was a bakery with a wood oven, and there were stables and a coal shed; going down the hill towards the Green was a small shed for corn, and I remember

Restall's 1928

Restall's 1960's

the doors eaten away at the bottom by the rats. The bins of corn were usually made of wood, so an awful lot of corn used to end up out in the road. There was a lovely grey carthorse and cart which Mr Greentree used to drive. He delivered all the goods from Restall's for many years. Then he drove a van and carried on with deliveries until he died. People didn't retire in those days. Restall's sold all sorts of things and also ran a Post Office. If anyone wanted some corn, the assistant had to leave everything, go down to the shed and weigh up the corn even on wet days, so it wasn't all honey serving in a shop, but the villagers have taken it all in their stride and the shop was still going strong with very good service in 1980. I remember sacks of sugar, rice, potatoes, oatmeal, etc. standing on the floor as one went in through a narrow doorway, over which hung hobnail boots, buckets and brushes, mostly for the farm workers.

Now the shed and stables are no more, and the land space has been given to a car park and houses.

Just down the hill by the pond were two cottages, one of which was Lynden Cottage. Doctor Rock used to have the front room at Lynden Cottage once a week to see anyone who was sick. When medicine was needed one paid 2s.6d. (12.5p) and he would make a bottle up while you waited. He lived at Hambledon.

Brooklyn House on the Hambledon Road, belonged to Febens. Mr Feben used to deliver coal, mostly on Saturdays, by horse and cart and later by lorry with the bags of coal all weighed and the scales at the back end. Each sack by law was supposed to be weighed before delivery, and it wasn't so good for the customer when it was raining, as the sacks got wet; then they weighed much heavier! Coal was used for all the heating in those days, as gas and electric never came to Denmead till the 1930's. The poor coalman always got so black with humping sacks of coal on his back, one didn't recognise him till Sunday when he would be in his Sunday best.

Not many people owned their own house in those days. There were no Council houses in Denmead, only private rented cottages, mostly farm cottages and a few houses in their own grounds. Some people used to live in train carriages which were down Edneys Lane and one or two by the Memorial Hall. Railway carriages made some very pretty dwellings as people would take a great pride in them and the garden surrounding them. The Terrace was built at the beginning of the last century and still stands today. The first six houses were built in 1893 and called 'The Shrubbery'; the other houses came later, with No. 38 being built in 1902.

Many naval people arrived in the village, as it was near enough to travel to Portsmouth each day for the men. The majority of thatched cottages went into disrepair and (thanks to the naval families) were bought and rebuilt into some lovely houses and now are in great demand. The character of the thatched cottages stands out, although being surrounded by newer type houses. Most old houses were built with flint stones which were collected from the dells in the fields, for example the school and the church.

If only one could look into the future, what fortunes we would make! Looking back into the past once again, come on down Anmore Road once again towards Lovedean. There's a big mansion house on the right towards Eastland Gate called Shrover Hall; it had a long drive to the house, and in the garden were many statues - "so ghostly", I thought. As a child we used to go to the Hall to buy apples, sixpence for a shopping-bag full and a small bag for each of us children given to us to eat on the way home. I remember a lovely magnolia tree near the door, and also opposite was an old chapel, where services used to be held when Sir William Pink lived there, but hadn't been in use in my lifetime. As children we were allowed in there and up the narrow stairs inside. It was used then for drying corn and storing apples.

At the back of Shrover Hall was a place where animals were slaughtered for meat, and I can remember very well the poor types of cattle grazing in the fields awaiting their doom, I never enjoyed going to Shrover Hall; but it had great attractions.

On the way back from there we would call at Anmore Dell, a real play area for children, usually half filled with water drained from all the surrounding fields. Such a big place it seemed, we could climb up banks and even swim in the water. Also there was always a crowd of ducks waiting to be fed from the picnic bags. You see it was as near to the seaside we could go in those days.

We would also call in at Shafters Farm, where the pigs were in sties and how fascinating to lean over the sties and talk to the pigs. The farmer, Mr Tilbury, was very fond of children and we were never grumbled at, and his dear wife used to show us the honeycombs from the bee hives; many a time she would give us a piece of honeycomb.

As we left the farm so we came to King's Pond which is, of course, still on the bend opposite King's Cottage which was also a farm but the pond was so overgrown we never used to go on it although I remember one year we had a hard winter and many villagers skated on it, and had much enjoyment doing so.

When we got to the crossroads there was a gravel pit up Mill Road, of course that has since been levelled up and built on, but the gardens are still very stony for the people who live there, Denmead ground seems to vary from clay, sand and gravel and lovely black soil; I think it was to do with the Ice Age. Also at Mill Road stood the Mill which was dismantled in 1922, but I believe a millstone is still there at Mill House.

In Soake Road was a sand pit. The sand was used a great deal during the War for sandbags for barricading against the bombs in the towns and built up areas. Most people would lend a hand in those days to fill a sand bag. Where the sand had been excavated water came and with it fish, so some people would go there to fish.

The village has grown and altered but also improved in many ways. Many more houses are being built each year, so bringing more roads and more people, but it still has that village life. The Village Hall on the Hambledon Road was built after the 1914 War as a memorial to the people who served in the Forces. The village couldn't really afford it at the time, and it took many years to pay off the debt.

It has been modernised and extended over the years and survived a fire in February 1990.

The Memorial Hall

A wartime Christmas dinner at the Memorial Hall
Bessie's mother Julia is seated third from right

We have had some marvellous times there and some very good amateur operatic shows have been held. During the War the Army took it over and soldiers had it as a dining hall and dormitory.

At the back of All Saints' Church was a nice sized wooden hut where festivities were held. The soldiers used it as a voluntary canteen run by voluntary workers from the Church and many a soldier was pleased to get a meal of an evening after being on manoeuvres out in the country for long hours at a time. It brought a little bit of home nearer to them by meeting the villagers and being invited to their homes of an evening. Some of the men married village girls and still live in the surrounding districts.

The Church Hut as it was has been pulled down and another one has been built there of brick.

The villagers bought a tile each for the roof and had their names put on them, as the old roofing tiles were re-used. The Church really plays a big part in village life and everything seems to revolve round it.

Even the church has been altered a bit; I remember the vestry at the eastern end by the altar, where a man or woman would ring the bells. We had two, and there used to be a boy who pumped the organ. We had a most wonderful organ for a village church, but it cost a lot of money for the upkeep, but somehow the villagers rallied around, and so the cost was found somehow.

All Saints' Church Bazaar, 1949 - with Julia Simmonds fifth from right front row

Many people who were born and lived in the village many years ago and have since moved away to other parts of the world never forget Denmead, although it may be years before they return. Of course Denmead wasn't always called Denmead, and it wasn't marked on the map for many years. It used to be called Barn Green, I believe, near Hambledon. Even after 50 years of absence travelling world-wide, Denmead has that magnetic appeal, 'home'.

It's the community life which is very strong even with so many houses going up each day. It started at the beginning of the settlement of farmers. Then came the Navy and the townspeople wanting homes in the country, usually at weekends. In Denmead we were like one big family, not much more than 30 years ago, and now it's all enlarged and the population has risen tremendously.

We don't know each other's names, but we recognise each other as we go to the village shops, and I guess everyone fits into village life. One need never be lonely. Just for the sake of looking out of doors, somebody will pass by and speak. It's a wonderful village to live in. No floods or earthquakes, or even bad weather, which is usually worse elsewhere.

Bessie's mother Julia Simmonds

My mother arrived here to live in 1905 and didn't unpack all the goods she brought with her for three years, as she never intended to stay, but stay she did and brought up eight children, being left a widow at 40. She died here when she was 80. She loved Denmead and only lived in Brooklyn Terrace, never even wanting to move to anything better. She was a well-loved figure in Denmead, and a devoted member of the church, and brought many a baby into the world, and even laid people to rest.

THE
Vicarage

Going to a village school was a recognised thing in a village for the working class which I belonged to. Having been born in 1921 and the youngest of eight children, my mother had brought up my five brothers and two sisters mostly without the aid of my father. Before I was born he was often away to sea for two or three years at a time. It wasn't until I was coming into the world that he retired from the Navy. My eldest sister was then eighteen years old and working at Waterlooville as a domestic general maid, a position suitable for all young girls in those days. I had two brothers at work also, and two other brothers and a sister at school, and my youngest brother was two years older than I, so he was still a toddler who needed looking after. My father on retirement from the Navy (he had risen to the rank of Chief Petty Officer-Chief Stoker, and had an excellent career) took a job at Rowlands Castle in the brickfields there to help give the family a good living, but it wasn't to be. I was just six weeks old, and having been born at Christmas the weather was at its wettest and coldest when my father caught the 'flu like many others at the time, and so died within about three days.

My mother then had to make her living and so carry on bringing up us children, which meant going out to work and taking in washing. Even then two of my brothers who attended Denmead School were sent up to Staffordshire to an orphanage until they were of an age at 14 years when they would come back to Denmead and take a job of work to help the family.

As I grew up I remember how heart-broken my mother was at times having to let my brothers go to an orphanage. I remember when they came home during holiday times in the summer, then having to go back to the orphanage again. At the time of my father's death his pension died with him and mother only had a very small amount to pay rent and an allowance for three of us while we went to school, but as soon as my sister left at 14 the few shillings the Government allowed for her was stopped, although she was still needing to be looked after. My sister then had to go to domestic work as was the custom. In any case no other type of work was available in the village in those days. Her first job was at the Vicarage also, and after a while she left and worked at other houses still doing domestic work.

My mother stayed many years with Vicar Green's family, although he died when I was aged about ten years. Mrs Green and her daughter moved to Waterlooville and mother used to go to their other house. My mother while she was working would receive about 3p per hour. Her tasks mainly were washing or scrubbing floors. She

Left to right: Beatrice (born 1903), Cecil, George (1912), Charles (1905), Julia Simmonds with Bessie (1921) on her lap, Doris, Sidney and Frederick
Bessie's father was superimposed on this family photo as he died six weeks after Bessie was born

was so grateful to think she had the health and strength to enable her to do so, and work from other people would come her way. I used to accompany her to the Vicarage each time she went and as I was growing up so I remember different happenings there.

I remember meeting Vicar Green, such a tall stately man as I thought, with pure white hair and dressed all in black. A man to be obeyed.

Vicar Green

I remember how he called through the hatchway from the dining room to the kitchen and spoke to me. I was rather shy then. I imagined him as Jesus would have been, with his white hair and smiling face, so gentle and very quiet-spoken. I was rather curious from then onwards what was the other side of the little door in the wall.

As I stood in the kitchen by the window along the far side of the kitchen, hung a row of bells, from large ones to a very small one which used to ring on occasion. They were bells on wire and made a rather nice sound. In those days besides my mother working at the Vicarage there were two other maids, one whose name was Mildred, I believe she used to do the cooking. I remember the large dresser with a set of brown jugs and the copper jugs which shone like mirrors. In those days the copper jugs were in use for carrying hot or cold water upstairs to the bedrooms, as no bathroom had been installed, although a very large combustion stove was used for heating upstairs on the landing. A hip bath of enamel would be taken into the bedrooms and filled with water for a weekly bath, and for daily washing a wash stand stood in each bedroom on which was a marble slab with a basin and bowl of beautiful designs of flowers printed on them, plus china jars for soap and tooth cleaning, etc. In the jug on the wash stand was cold water which was always in use whatever the temperature, as hot water was a luxury and only brought to the bedroom if asked for.

Two of the bedrooms although large had a dressing room next to them. I remember going up the back stairs from the kitchen (servants weren't allowed to use the main staircase). They were white scrubbed wood which had a twist in them and were rather narrow. It was after I left school and started work at 14 for Reverend Miller and his family that I fell down on those same stairs while carrying a large bucket of hot water with which to scrub them. Luckily as they weren't covered in any way the water was soon absorbed into the wood and I was none the worse for it.

The Reverend Hubert Miller

While I was a very small child Vicar Green's daughter Mrs Tooker became ill for quite a long while and had to take to her bed. It was then I used to be able to go and talk to her in her bedroom. I was privileged to play there with a most beautiful doll and cradle which belonged to her daughter Ann, who then was away at boarding school. I was also given a small wooden clock for myself, but alas after taking it home it eventually was investigated by my elder brothers, so in the end the clock was no more, but I will always remember my first clock. After that I had many little toys given me from Mrs Tooker. When I attended Church Sunday School Mrs Tooker then was my teacher. I was about nine years old then, I had been attending Chapel from the time I could walk, but I wanted to start Church as I had a friend who used to go. My mother encouraged me to do so on the understanding that I would attend regularly, for which I did, and I was rewarded by a present of a book one year and a picture the next, which I treasured for many years.

I found the Sunday School a lot different from attending Chapel. For one thing a Children's Corner was to be seen at the back of the Church where candles were lit at each meeting, lighting up a beautiful picture of Jesus with prints of birds and beasts of the field. I still see that picture in my mind today, and I also remember the words surrounding it: "All Things Bright and Beautiful, All Creatures Great and Small" etc. As I was nine years old then, I went to Sunday School in the Church, but for the younger children Sunday school was held in the Church Hut: a wooden barrack-type hut used in wartime for the troops. Miss Chamberlain taught the younger ones. Each week she would walk from near World's End to take the Sunday School Service. She was so devoted, and a person to respect by us children.

1st Waterlooville Guides - Bessie would cycle to Waterlooville on her sister's bicycle

At Christmas she would arrange to show us in the hut a scene of the Birth of Christ which was beautifully modelled and we would stand back and look at it all the time as she read The Christmas Story. Each year it was wrapped up and put away again till the next Christmas. I was very happy with going to Church and I carried on going till I grew up and left the village to go in the ATS at 19 years old.

Pantomime in the Memorial Hall, Christmas 1935
'Babes in the Wood and Bold Robin Hood' - Bessie is in black dressed as Friar Tuck
The Panto travelled to other villages

I left school just a week before I was 14, at Christmas 1935. A job of work had already been chosen for me. It was at the Vicarage to work for the new Vicar Reverend Miller. He was new to the village, having come from Cowplain recently losing his wife, leaving him with three sons and two daughters who were growing up and so came with him. I started on Monday morning before Christmas, as I left school on the Friday being 14 years old on December 18th. It seemed a great hardship for me to have to start as a general maid, and not even have a holiday after leaving school. Still it was soon forgotten and I began to really believe I was grown up. I was paid 4/6 (22.5p) the first week and if I was suitable I could stay on and receive 5/- (25p) per week, out of that I had to give my mother 1/- (5p) each week plus coppers to pay for my laundry which she did for me. At that time laundry was a big thing. You see I had to wear a uniform which was black stockings and shoes, morning cap and apron and a royal blue dress just for the morning, then change in the afternoon to another dress with a very pretty cap and afternoon apron of broderie anglais. Aprons and caps had to be starched and perfectly white. When I did any scrubbing or seeing to the fires I would also put on a coloured apron on top.

Well, I started work and I was allotted a bedroom at the back of the house upstairs in the servants' quarters all on my own shut off by a door to the main landing and bedrooms. I slept in a large room which had bars up at the window (it used to be a nursery) with a very small fireplace: just a bed and a chair and lino on the floor, no mat or any other furniture. I lived out of my suitcase which I was so proud to possess, my mother having bought it specially for me.

Next to the nursery (come bedroom) was a bathroom, the only one in the house. I wasn't allowed to use it as it was for use of the family. A toilet was there though which I had permission to use. The very twisted stairs from the small landing led down into the kitchen and outside in the out-houses a toilet was next to the coal and wood shed.

I used to awake in the morning at 6 o'clock by an alarm clock which seemed to sound so loud and empty. I began to get very used to it though. My first tasks then would be to light the fire in the kitchen, a stove with ovens and hot water. It usually lit OK, but sometimes I failed to get any heat from it. There was an electric cooker and water heater over the sink in the scullery, so then I would proceed to carry hot water jugs to each bedroom up the backstairs. I was never allowed on the large stairs, only to clean them, which like the landing and all the floors throughout (except the kitchen part) were all highly polished with O'Cedar oil, and rugs placed at intervals on them.

My worst job I found was lighting the dining room fire. I used to spend hours trying to get the fire to burn, but not always with success. I used to have to use rolls of newspaper very often without any wood to light the fire, as wood was never bought, only gathered from the large orchard which was on the left hand side of the driveway going towards the church. The wood would be damp and needed to be chopped and broken up, which I used to have to do. After lighting the fire I would then prepare and cook the breakfast which always started with oatmeal which had to be soaked overnight, then water was taken up in jugs to the bedrooms.

Breakfast time I would sound a large brass gong by beating with a small hammer, then the Vicar with his family would arrive in the dining room. After the meal I would be asked into the dining room for morning prayer. Reverend Miller sitting at the head of the table, would read a piece from the great Bible.

Thus the day would begin. Miss Miller and myself then saw to all the household chores which were of many varieties including collecting vegetables and fruit from the garden, making jams and pickles and she would teach me to cook and how to do many useful jobs in home-making.

Reverend Miller also kept hives of bees and I would often help him when he opened them up very often holding the corrugated cardboard which was lit to make the smoke to keep off the bees. Life at the Vicarage was very enjoyable as many people would visit each day with their problems, and as Reverend Miller's sons and daughters were growing up so at times parties would take place.

I especially liked Easter Sunday after attending Morning Service. In the afternoon eggs were hidden in all the hedges round the garden and I was allowed to join the family and guests and search for them.

During the winter, parties and games would take place in the Coach House where there was a loft. Outside the kitchen buildings, I remember a yew tree which a barn owl often flew from to the barn as I was walking along the pathway, which used to frighten me very much as I used to be very frightened of owls, having heard of such terrible things about them when I was younger.

Also bats used to fly about each evening. I remember waking up one night with bats flying in my bedroom. I had left the window open. Of course I screamed out and Reverend Miller came to the rescue and sent the bats out through the window. After that episode my window would be closed.

In the Village Hall each month Miss Miller would hold a Church Social evening. A very popular event, sandwiches and cakes were supplied free with the cost of entry ticket. How the villagers enjoyed it, young and old. The first half up to 10 p.m. would be games, and the second half was ballroom dancing. This event lasted for a few years till the War finished and things began to take on a different aspect. Many a person still can remember the Church Socials.

So life went on in a very pleasant leisurely way, I stayed working at the Vicarage for 18 months, when I left to go on to do housework elsewhere, but not before I had found another girl who could take my place.

OPERATION
Tonsils
1927

As a child of about six, the time had come when I had to have my tonsils out, which meant going into hospital. Maybe many people would say that would be an everyday occurrence in the medical world of today, but my experience took place in the nineteen-twenties when surgery was a lot different in procedure than today.

I didn't know anything about entering hospital, as my mother never mentioned about it until I arrived with her in the Eye and Ear Hospital in Southsea, what a frightening experience! As far as I remember a neighbour accompanied my mother and I.

We boarded a little grey bus, to take us into Portsmouth. We then had some walking to do. I remember the bus we travelled in was owned by Charlie Briggs from Hambledon, I think he ran the bus to and fro to Portsmouth on certain days of the week, I suppose it would have held about eight passengers.

In those days there was no definite bus stops so people would be able to board the bus anywhere along the route. I believe when we arrived in the town we went round Woolworth's being a rather attractive store, where everything one was able to buy in the store would cost no more than sixpence in old money, so it was known as the sixpenny store where many families would spend a great deal of money rather than spend elsewhere. I remember choosing a celluloid doll which stood about six inches high, dressed in a coloured feathered skirt like a Red Indian, I think perhaps the colour of the feathers rather attracted me to it. It never closed its eyes or was able to move its legs but I clenched it in my hand lovingly as if it was a great treasure.

Afterwards we walked, to the hospital. I well remember taking hold of my mother's hand and with my other hand taking hold of my neighbour's hand. I then amused myself as we walked along by trying not to walk on the cracks and the joins in the pavement. I had never walked on paving stones along a road before, as living in Denmead we only had rough roads and grass verges.

Eventually we arrived at the hospital. I remember going into a big room where there were nurses dressed in uniform. I began to feel very frightened not sure of what was to happen to me so I began to cry. I was then shown into a room where boys and girls were happily playing with toys. I was promised that I would be able to play in the room later, but when I looked around my mother and neighbour had vanished!

I cried again and made a big scene and eventually I was lifted up to a window to see if I was able to see my mother but to no avail. I guess I must have quietened down and was put into a bed in a ward with other boys and girls. I do not remember much else until I was with some more children when we were each holding a large coloured card, and sitting on a wooden bench outside the operating theatre. We were called in one at a time, there were some nurses and doctors standing around in the room when I went in, and I couldn't help notice the strong smell of chloroform. I then noticed a long type of bed, where I was then lifted and told to lay flat down on it. I believe my head rested on some sort of metal dish, while laying flat on my back. I looked up into a very bright light above my head which was so powerful I had to keep my eyes closed. Then a spray was placed over my whole face and the smell of the ether rendered me unconscious. I woke up later as I was being carried by people. We were ascending a staircase, which then led back up to the ward, where I was once more put to bed, I could see lots of blood then, and I could feel the pillow case of red rubber.

I eventually woke up to my surroundings, I was back in the same ward with the other children, my throat was hurting very much, so I asked the nurse as she came over to my bed if I might have some water. She then gave me a small glass of liquid which tasted so sweet that I asked for more, but one glass was all that I was allowed. Before long I was able to see around me to notice that the other children were quite lively and passing round to each other comics and books. Later a nurse came round to each bed holding a large syringe and syringed the children's ears. She approached my bed I began to be frightened thinking that my ears would be syringed also, but she only smiled as she passed me by. I think I then began to want to go home and began to ask for my mother. I fell asleep once more, it must have been the next day when I woke to find my mother had come back to see me and she was in the ward where I was. After a conversation with the doctor it was arranged for me to get dressed, and to go with my mother back home to Denmead. First of all my mother opened her shopping bag and gave the nurse in charge bananas and eggs for the other children in the ward which the hospital was very grateful to receive. We travelled home once more in the grey bus for the ten miles back to Denmead. I remember it was a fine day and the sun was shining bright.

My throat was still hurting me and Mr Briggs the driver and owner of the bus decided to stop the bus in the town and my mother stepped off the bus, went into a shop and came back with ice cream for each of us. I am sure I really felt a lot better then realising I was actually going back home. When we alighted from the bus my brother and sister were there to meet us, being very excited to see me once more, they couldn't stop talking until we arrived indoors, when my brother showed me what he had made for me while I was away. Made from a cardboard shoe box, it was a make-believe theatre with scenery and cut out figures as the actors and even a small light inside from a torch which gave it a sense of realism.

WHAT A HOMECOMING! It seemed such a long time I had been in hospital, but in reality it was less than a week, but how it altered our relationship by being apart, what fun we had with the shoe box and what a homecoming I had!

Sundays

Sunday had come round again, not an important one, but when I woke up this morning my mind went back to my childhood days, many years ago, when I was the youngest of eight children living with my mother in a 3-up 3-down terrace house in a village in Hampshire.

My father who was in the Navy had died when I was born, so mum kept the home going. We weren't all living at home at the same time, I had two brothers away in an orphanage till they were 14 years old and could then come home and go out to work. An elder sister was away in domestic service, and another brother had left home to seek his fortune in New Zealand when he was just 18, which left four of us and mother. Charlie my eldest brother took over most of the outdoor work, gardening etc., which left mum time to look after us in the house.

Saturday night was bath night for us younger ones, us two girls would bath first then my young brother all in the same bath water in the bath on the mat in front of the firestove. Usually mother would bath us after putting in extra hot water from the stove for each of us. After bathing my eldest brother Charlie would then enter back into the house and mum and Charlie would then carry the bath out into the yard with all the water in, which would stay outside till the next morning.

Well, Sunday morning was different from any other day as we would start the day with our best clothes on in readiness to go to Chapel for morning service and afternoon Sunday School.

Bessie with little Ronnie and her white angora rabbit

First of all after we came downstairs Mum would be cooking our breakfast. Most Sundays we had boiled smoked haddock; one large haddock would be cut up in pieces and there was enough for each of us. The bread would have to be cut from the breadboard with a great deal of butter on a slice. Kettles would be boiling on the range, also the potato peelings were boiling in an iron saucepan for the purpose of feeding our dozen chickens each morning which were in a hen house down the bottom of the garden. Summer time or winter we had to have the fire going, as in those days we had no electricity or gas (which sometimes made a lot of work). I remember as I walked outside our back door on my way to our only toilet, I would see the bath of water from the night before which was waiting to be emptied. Very often black soot would be floating on the top of the water. My mother would be busy straining the potatoes from the saucepan into a colander then placing them into a bowl to be mixed up with some meal which used to be kept just inside our coalshed. Then I would have the privilege of helping to feed the chickens and look for the eggs. Our cat, Fluff, would also come in for a share of chicken food halfway down the path where mum would feed her a spoonful. We also had rabbits and they had to have a share, as well as having their 'greens'. Charlie in the meanwhile had gone to our allotment one mile away on his bike and would return home with the vegetables for our Sunday dinner. That meant bringing them home in a sack on the bars of his bicycle. By the time my brother arrived home mother would be ready to wash all the vegetables ready to prepare for cooking. During the summer garden peas had to be shelled plus broad beans which usually us children would undertake to do, potatoes being new would need the mud washed off and then scraped. Cabbage was another vegetable to contend with, the outer leaves had to be removed and the stumps cut off and given to the chickens. Eventually everything was in readiness to be cooked on the kitchen range in time for one o'clock dinner. We children would attend 11 a.m. service and arrive home just after 12 midday, usually with a small text in our hands given to us by the Sunday School teacher.

We would all take our places sitting up to the table where the dinner would be served. My mother would carve the meat if my eldest brother wasn't about and we would be served according to our ages. Mother also helped us younger ones to veg and gravy. A roast dinner was the thing for every family on a Sunday, living down South; a dinner which included three or four veg as well as meat and suet pudding which was boiled in water sometimes with the cabbage. The suet pudding was rolled up longwise wrapped in a cloth. If it was too much to eat we would then have the leftovers fried the next day and was so named 'Bubble and Squeak'. The suet pudding was eaten for afters served with golden syrup or jam and greatly enjoyed by all the family. Another way of serving plain suet pudding was to slice it and fry in the pan eating it hot served with a sprinkle of sugar.

Once dinner was over the children up to fourteen years would all be washed and dressed to go to the Sunday School at the Chapel nearby, or Church. In the meanwhile mother would go upstairs for a rest and usually came back downstairs when it was time for the children to arrive back home. Mother always put on her Sunday best dress and starched clean apron, also bringing with her from upstairs a pure white linen tablecloth for Sunday tea.

Sunday tea was a rather grand occasion as sometimes visitors would be calling in. We would all then sit on chairs round the large table which held a large cut-and-come-again cake, a dish of stewed fruit and bowl of custard, a large amount of white bread and butter also perhaps a plate of jam tarts and small rock cakes. Sometimes tinned fruit would be served instead of stewed, but that may have only happened near a birthday or Christmas.

After washing up and clearing away the meal and if we had visitors, it was often the thing to go for a walk. Being in the country most of our visitors would have to go with us to see part of the village also the lanes and our allotment of which we were rather proud. Of course on a Sunday the village would be a quiet place with no traffic and most villagers standing by the doors of their cottages, would come out to greet you as one passed along the road. Sometimes we would stop and talk to people we hadn't seen for a while, and it would soon be getting dark by the time we arrived home and our visitors would be boarding a bus to go back to the town loaded with a large bunch of flowers plus a few vegetables, and very grateful for their day out, waiting till, perhaps, another year, maybe, before we would see them again.

So Sunday ended and Monday would soon be once more on us, when we younger ones went in the morning to school.

How times have changed!

COUNTRY
Born and Bred

As a child brought up in the 1920's I think how lucky I was being able to live in the country. The way of life as I saw it, being entirely different for a country child, compared with the upbringing of children living in the town.

One of my first recollections was playing with other children of mixed age groups in the field opposite my home. We never seemed to stay in our own gardens, for one thing, we weren't allowed to get on the garden, because of the cultivation of the vegetables. We had no lawn, just one or two clumps of perennial flowers up near the house, and down the bottom of the garden chickens were kept in a run. The gardens were not fenced off and so as a child we would run up and down other neighbours' garden paths respecting the gardens and never walking on them.

It was very interesting playing in the field. Such a lot would be going on and such a lot to learn. I remember often sitting on the grass in little groups in the summer making daisy chains, an older child having shown the younger ones what to do, picking the daisies and making a slit with our little fingers so enabling the next daisy to be pulled through. Then when the daisy chain was made so we would decorate ourselves up in flowers and run around singing and dancing imagining we were in fairyland.

In those days we had such long summers where looking back the sun was always shining. There was so much to do each day we never thought the summer would end. I remember lying in the grass, we were so small and the grass was so very high and would soon hide a child. It was a lovely game playing at hiding in the grass. Often a grown-up would come by and not see us. I remember how the boys used to climb trees, even a girl would attempt it as well, but that would be frowned upon as girls had different clothes on, whereas boys would often tear their trousers and end up with a hiding for doing so. Eventually the trousers were worn by them again with a great big patch in the back often of a different colour. Girls may have torn their dresses and petticoats and had to mend them their own selves.

We often would walk round the field looking for birds' nests. Children would take an egg but it was a rule only one egg to be taken from a nest. Many a child had a collection of wild birds' eggs. There were dog roses in profusion growing in the hedgerows and how we used to reach up to pick the honeysuckle and often pull the petals out and suck from them the honey. Wild flowers are so lovely growing in their own environment. What child could resist the gathering of them to take as a present home to their mothers? The first celandine growing in the ditches as winter was nearing its end, wild snowdrops and later bluebells, water buttercups, anemones and Solomon's seal and the little blue dog violets, even white and red ones would be found if one knew where to look.

How lovely the bluebells looked when they were growing in the woods so like a blue carpet against the greenery of the trees and then to see the anemones showing up white and they would need picking as well. How lucky we would feel if we happened to find Solomon's seal with the little flowers hanging from the stem. Very often we would take the flowers home and they would end up in a row of jam jars on the kitchen windowsills inside and out, but the bluebells with the Solomon's seal would be in a vase on the polished front room table in all their glory.

Besides the picking of flowers there was the harvest of food from the fields and hedges, such as blackberries, crab apples and nuts and elderberries. We would be encouraged to gather such goodies to take home as each fruit was of good value healthwise. How lovely to eat blackberry and apple pie and in cold weather partake of elderberry wine!

Mushrooms came at different seasons of the year. We knew which ones to pick and what not to, like the poisonous berries in the hedges and ditches. The knowledge had been handed down from generation to generation, the older children teaching the younger ones. Nuts were eaten on the way to school; mainly walnuts which meant looking for them on the ground after a stormy night, picking up the black looking shucks and smashing them open by one's foot to find the walnut inside. Then having to break open the shell and there find the kernel covered in yellow skin which had to be peeled off as it tasted so bitter; by then the nut tasted delicious but our hands which started off so clean would be stained brown. It was unheard of to climb trees for nuts, we only ever had ones that fell to the ground.

I remember attending school each day at Denmead. I lived a mile away but it was a very interesting walk each day there and back.

First of all we would meet outside the Terrace, other children lived further back towards Lovedean. Now they would have had to be up early to get to school by 8.45. We would all go together, boys and girls all ages from 5 to 14 years old running and shoving each other playing ball or rolling a hoop, the boys kicking a ball about until it got lost in a hedge. We would first arrive at Restall's and the smell of the bakery would hit our nostrils and tempt our appetites. We usually spent our halfpennies on the way to school in Restall's; we would go to buy an ounce of toffees which worked out about eight toffees or boiled sweets, sometimes liquorice bootlaces or gobstoppers. Gobstoppers lasted all the way to school. They were sucked and as they melted in our mouths another colour would arrive on them, and it seemed like magic sweets to us children.

Anthill Common School, 1920's - Bessie is third from right

Sometimes we were able to buy a pennyworth of broken biscuits for our midday lunch or penny packets of broken crisps, such luxuries! Well, we would then proceed towards the pond after warming our hands on a hotplate fixed on the wall near the bakery.

When we arrived at the pond we would then dare each other to go near the water to look for frog's jelly and other interesting things. We would be daring and walk on the inside of the railings along a foot-wide wall. Sometimes one child would push another then perhaps a child would almost slip into the mud and water. After leaving the pond we might wander off to the village green where Miss Wakeford's shop was. As one entered through the double door a bell would ring overhead and out through the back of the shop Miss Wakeford would come to serve us. I remember the glass boxes the length of the counter in which were laid all the sweets and toffees only children appreciated, but come near firework time November 5th and those glass cases would contain all sorts of fireworks, bangers and sparklers. Many a child would save up to buy fireworks to celebrate Guy Fawkes Day. As we left Miss Wakeford's, our next port of call was the blacksmiths, to see him make horseshoes, hammering and heating the metal, the fire dying down to black then he would pump the bellows and the fire would be alive again with sparks flying like fireworks. Sometimes a horse would be waiting there to be shod.

I remember to this day standing with other children pushing and shoving trying to look over the halfway door watching the smithy lifting the horse's hoof and then proceeding to shoe the horse.

We used to be very concerned about the poor horse and the smell of the hoof as the hot shoe was being nailed to his foot, but all was well and the horse would be

The Village Green, showing Miss Wakeford's shop to the left and The Smithy on the far right

ready to go on the road again. It seemed ages we would be standing there when suddenly the sound of the school bell was ringing out loud and clear so away towards school we went without any more hanging about.

On our way back home at a quarter to four would be more adventures. We were taught in those days always to walk on the left hand side. If there was a pavement then walk on the pavement, but coming home from school there was Harts Copse which was quite an attraction. So much rubbish from village cottages had been dumped just inside the gate that it was like treasure trove, or so we thought. We would often pick up some 'treasure' there for our parents. What reason we would carry it home for I do not know 'cos when we arrived home it would be taken from us and disposed of!

Sometimes we would venture further into the woods by the pathways; one led to a big dell where we could play for hours climbing up the sides and sliding down the banks. We used to spend many hours in those woods and eventually leave the woods and walk on through the allotments and then on taking a cut across the field to go through the churchyard.

As we walked through the paths of the allotments we might see rhubarb growing and as we were hot and thirsty so we would carefully steal a stick of rhubarb which would be shared between us knowing it tasted better because we had pulled it.

We could go another way home instead of keeping on the Hambledon Road, we would turn off on the right down a small lane now called Green Lane which then was known as Harrison's Lane. On the corner would be a game of tennis being

The allotment of Bessie's first husband Mr Greenaway

played in those days, the men were in grey or white flannels and white shirts and the ladies always in a white outfit. We would stay a while to watch the tennis, and then go further on to the old yew tree where we could climb in and out of its trunk. Being so old it was of such interest to us as children, I was told it was mentioned in the Doomsday Book; nearby is a large house called Shere which I believe was also mentioned. As we came to Southwick Road we turned left and then just nearby on the right was Ashling House, not so very many years old but very stately, the walls were of flintstones and lovely great windows shining out onto parkland with large sycamore and oak trees and large lawns where fêtes and flower shows were held annually. A farm was at the end of the large high flint wall which surrounded it, with a farm cottage nearby. We would pick up handfuls of beechnuts from the beech trees overhanging the wall.

At the end of Ashling House which is now Ashling Park Road was a cart track where two chestnut trees stood in the middle of the entrance and we used to spend hours searching for conkers.

As we wended our way home we would get nearer to the Forest of Bere and in view was the Dando wheel shining bright with the evening sun shining on the blades. We had arrived home from school back to the Terrace and a good meal would be ready for us.

As we stayed at school all day we would have a hot meal of lamb stew or sometimes meat and veg followed by milk puddings. Now to be able enjoy a milk pudding, each evening most children took their milk cans up to the local farm which for us in the Terrace would be at Mr Stares. We would buy one pint and a half of separated milk at one penny a pint, the milk puddings would turn out delicious. Sometimes we would get rabbit pie, rabbits in those days were often on the menu costing only about one shilling each. Then, I remember, one could cure the fur skins which would make a nice mat by the side of the bed. Also the skins would improve a child's coat by providing a fur collar and cuffs; even fur-backed gloves would be made from rabbits' fur. After tea we would go out to play again; mostly games played out in the road as we seldom got a car down the road in the evening. Horses and carts would have done their work for the day except if it was harvest or haymaking time. Then we all would hurry to the hayfields and play in the hay as the farmer allowed us to do the tossing of hay which helped to dry it.

Anthill School - early days

Holidays were days to be looked forward to. Although we never travelled far, we always went to the seaside on our annual Sunday School Treat. Then we would leave about 9 in the morning and after boarding a charabanc we would be in another world for the day. Mother would be waiting for us when we arrived home. We would be sunburnt and tired with the change of air, but what a day to be remembered. Our bucket we took to the seaside would be carefully carried on the charabanc and taken to the kitchen window sills when we arrived home, full of seaweed, shells and sand, sometimes crabs. Then the seaweed, our 'Weather Forecaster' would be hung up on a nail by the back door near the fir cones we had collected at different times in Denmead. The window sill outside was always used for our treasures that we would bring home.

I suppose it's a natural thing for children to have possessions. I remember my brother as a young boy would have his pockets bulging at times with marbles, string, penknife and many other assorted items, all very useful to him. Pieces of chalk were to be found at various places in Denmead and as children we would always be using chalk not only on a piece of slate but for marking our heights on walls and certain games on the road, like jumping and hopscotch. Chalk marks seemed to be everywhere where children played. If a child chalked on a wall or fence the householders would come out and reprimand the child then supply cleaning-off material for the culprit to clean the chalk off. Very often a child got away with it, so the householder ended up by cleaning it off themselves.

Most homes especially along the Terrace boasted a front door step which every morning or so would be scrubbed and then whitened with a large piece of chalk. The chalk was usually brought home from a walk to Pithill. As children we would be tempted to place our feet on a clean surface and make marks, so the housewife would then have to wipe the step over again. I remember outside the Forest of Bere a newly cemented forecourt was laid and passing children walked on it, with different sized feet, the marks are still there now.

Inside a house would be a cooking range with a white hearth, chalk again was used and also a copper used for boiling clothes would be chalked over.

As children we walked miles during the holidays roaming the countryside, our parents never set eyes on us from morning till evening when we would arrive home tired and hungry. Often we would take cold tea in a bottle or homemade lemonade, but we would soon drink up and then wait till we got home again for the next drink. Sometimes we would call at a cottage for a glass of water and with great excitement we were able to peer down a well while a bucket of water was being drawn up.

As the days grew shorter so our activities outside would alter. Then we would attend Chapel of an evening to see a Magic Lantern Service. How exciting, we used to sit in darkness watching a lighted screen as the camera showed us pictures of places we had only heard of in the Bible. A story would be read to us explaining the different scenes, but all those stories were so sad but they brought home to us how other people lived and survived.

It usually left us with food for thought. As we came out once more into the moonlight we would often walk with grown-ups to see other children back to their homes further in the village. Then we would be able to see the stars picking out all the pictures in the sky which the pattern of the stars made. Sometimes we even saw a shooting star, then everybody would send up a cheer saying "Look, another baby is born!"

Sometimes we would spend an evening in other children's houses playing Ludo, cards or draughts, and the parents would see us back home safely.

Before Christmas arrived we would go out in groups up and down the roads carol singing. Everyone knew everybody in the village in those days, so often we would be invited in for a piece of cake or mince pie to sing to a housebound person whose only entertainment was listening to the singing. Radio wasn't very much in vogue in those days and certainly TV was unheard of. We were never encouraged to sing for money; if we needed money we found we had to work for it, like running errands to the shops or delivering washing to the big houses.

Money wasn't the main thing in life then. We were much happier in the country without it.

Brooklyn Terrace with Baptist Chapel in the background

We were rich with the harvest of the countryside. There was always a fire in our homes, we never went cold as the families would go wooding and we never knew what it was to go hungry, as there would always be meat and eggs and milk and as regards vegetables everyone had a garden which would grow all what was needed and more besides. Children of my age never had many bought toys. Most amusements were home made. Cardboard boxes were so very useful and would keep us occupied with the things that a child could make from them. Books and dolls were usually given to us from a Sunday School Christmas Tree according to our attendance. Some things like hoops, skipping ropes and balls would be bought in the family then handed down to younger ones, but they would last us a long time even then they eventually got passed on to another family who might be worse off than us.

When it came to Christmas and gifts were distributed, one could see they were home made with great pride from the giver. Children had been busy weeks ahead making things with wood or needleworking. Every householder would get a kettleholder and pincushion; things like that were so very useful and were in use daily.

So in the country it was a happy and contented life for many children who never knew any different ways of living in their young lives, till perhaps people from the town would move into a house nearby and tell us their ways of life.

WASHING DAY
In the 30's

If there was one day of the week I disliked most it was Monday when I was a child. Of course it was the start of another school week, which was quite nice really especially after a weekend at home with my brothers and sisters. They were all older than I and their interests were unknown to me at the time. My father having died with the 'flu soon after I was born, was only a name in the family, so my mother being my only parent would often seek help from my elder brother whom I respected very much and looked upon as a father figure. So being the youngest of eight, I guess I was a little bit spoilt and tended to go my own way very often. My other brother, two years my senior would often tease me and so make my days a little bit harder to bear. It wasn't all peace and harmony. We often would argue and have a few tears but nevertheless we thought a great deal of each other.

It would be Monday mornings we didn't agree very much, you see it was WASHING DAY.

My mother would rise very early in the morning, seeing her older children off to work which then left my brother and I waiting to go to school, but first the jobs had to be done. Water for washday had first to be collected in buckets from the pump. Now the pump stood between two houses a few doors away, and the water was pumped out by anybody who needed it. In our row of twenty-one houses there were three such pumps, each supplying seven houses. The water came from a dando which was a well with tanks above, large pipes going down a long way into the earth, and a large wheel driven by the wind which was fixed high above the tanks. Sometimes the wheel would blow off into someone's garden and cause much damage, then we had no water to use, as water from the dando was also connected for use in each house. So whoever arrived at the pump first would use the handle, pump up and down and the water would then gush out into a bucket. Of course one had to watch very carefully in case the water would splash over their feet or down their clothes. My brother and I between us would then carry a bucket of water back to the house for my mother, enabling her to fill the large iron copper which was set in cement in the corner of the scullery near the sink. A fire hole was built in the front and underneath the copper, and when the water was emptied into the copper, a fire was lit using paper, rubbish and wood, sometimes a little coal to get it going, then adding any household refuse such as worn out shoes and boots and even vegetable peelings.

Very often we went for another bucket of water perhaps by then other children of our neighbours would be getting their water like us, as it was customary for everyone to wash their clothes always on a Monday, and that meant we would need to stand and wait our turn, but somehow we managed to arrive at school on time.

While we were at school my mother would then work very hard at the washing. First of all, the copper after being filled with water from the pump would have the fire lit underneath to boil it.

In the meanwhile waiting for the copper to get hot and come to the boil, mother would bring in the large bath of galvanised tin from the wall outside the backyard and also a small bath which she used for rinsing with Reckitt's Blue Bag swished round in the clear water to give the clothes a whiter look once they had been washed. She washed the clothes in the big bath, then transferred all the whites to the copper for boiling, then the rinsing bath was stood underneath the mangle, another bath was on the floor catching the water as the clothes were put through the mangle.

Our mangle I remember was about four feet in height and had a big iron frame with two wooden rollers

French advert for Reckitt's 'Blue' Bag

of eight inches in diameter and about a two-and-a-half feet in width, and as a person turned the handle of the large wheels so the rollers would turn the washing back or forward according to which way the wheels were turned. It was interesting work watching the big wheels going round and the water gushing out.

There was no protection or covers on the machine cogs and works, and dust would easily collect on the mangle which usually needed to be wiped down before and again after use to stop the rust going onto the clothes.

In those days using rainwater was the ideal thing as it was lovely and soft and so we didn't need to use so much soap. The soap we used was a yellow block called 'Sunlight' and had to be cut up into smaller pieces for economy sake. Soap powder was of poor quality and so soda would be mainly in use, also ammonia and sometimes cooking salt to get stains out.

With much rubbing on a board and soaking and boiling, the clothes would be clean enough to hang out on the highest line which stretched out between posts the whole length of the back garden, propped up by a clothes prop which was a pole with a forked end.

Sometimes our neighbours would see the difference in the whiteness of each other's washing and so there was great competition as to who was the best laundry woman. Many housewives took in extra washing from the big houses as there wasn't much work about and the money for washing would help to supplement the household expenditure.

Yes, Monday was a very busy day. When the washing dried it would then have to be collected from the line in a wicker basket, oblong or oval in shape, carried under one's arm. Then clothes would be damped down and rolled ready for ironing the next day. Of course after the clothes were hung out, the waste water had to be disposed of by means of emptying all the receptacles and taken to the garden and emptied, throwing the water over the garden, as we never had any drains in the Terrace. Under the sink the water would often overflow from the pipe into the already filled-up bucket underneath, which was always being forgotten. So the floor which was of cement would have to be scrubbed and then the copper raked out and the copper which had previously been used would need to be emptied and dried and the cement wall would then be whitened each week with chalk and water, then left with its wooden lid and copper stick up on the top to dry out. All this, part of the Monday washday, would be happening as we were arriving from school in the afternoon. I would come running round the alley and the steam of washing would still smell and my spirits sank as I realised it was still washing day.

I would arrive at the back door as my mother would be on her hands and knees scrubbing the doorstep, and so that meant I wasn't allowed in right away. Newspaper would have to be placed on the floor first to dry up the damp, also in case our shoes made the floor muddy. Then eventually the old mats would be replaced and we would be allowed in.

Tea would be ready for us very soon after arriving home, and so I was able to go out and play before dark. Then a main meal would be cooked and ready in time for my brothers when they arrived later.

Being Monday the meal would consist of leftovers from Sunday's dinner. That would consist of cold lamb or beef with vegetables and potatoes fried in a pan till brown, called 'Bubble and Squeak'. If we needed any more to eat there was cold suet pudding which we used to eat with treacle on it; sometimes we would have it fried. Even to this day I will always remember those Mondays and I still detest 'Bubble and Squeak'.

BANK HOLIDAY MONDAY AT
Portsdown Hill

It was in the 1930's I remember the Fair being held each Bank Holiday: an event which hundreds of people from Portsmouth and the villages from over the hill would all attend. I remember the steam engines with their wheels of steel, and the smell of coal fires, and the steam coming from the funnels as they travelled along the London Road towards Portsdown, towing vans, and trailers, seeing the painted parts of roundabouts, the side shows, and the travellers themselves shouting and running beside them, guiding them into the opening on the hill.

How exciting to see the first of the caravans and trucks arrive on the hill, wondering how big the Fair would be. Would there be swinging boats, chair-a-planes, and two roundabouts? We just had to have patience and wait. Sometimes there was great difficulty in getting the vehicles onto the grass, owing perhaps to a wet summer or just a drop of rain overnight, but somehow the traction engines managed to get every vehicle parked in their positions.

Then came the erecting of the side shows and the roundabouts, which we loved to watch as the show people were kept busy with all their vehicles in use and each family giving their helping hands. It seemed ages before the Bank Holiday activities got started, although perhaps it might only have been the day before they had arrived on the Hill.

Gradually many people seemed to congregate around looking in amazement at the most colourful painted lorries and trailers and then watching the people unloading and erecting the roundabouts and side shows, etc; while the steam engines would puff and blow away on the side, for the generating of electricity to drive the motors for the music and workings of the roundabouts.

Long cables trailing along the ground from engines to caravans, and to side shows and cables overhead from pole to pole for the many lights which would brighten the sky, and would be seen from a great distance for the evening festivities.

Tough strong working men handling the pieces, fitting them together, till at last the roundabouts, chair-a-planes, swinging boats and side shows would all be created by these wonderful people who had arrived from who knows where. So quickly and efficiently they worked as families and as a team, their skills handed down from generation to generation.

At last Bank Holiday had arrived!

The people began to arrive in the morning, climbing the hill above the Fair, to get the grand view overlooking Portsmouth and the Fair, to picnic and wait till the Fair got under way. The music would start, the bright lights would shine and then the side shows would open up for business and so the Fair got under way.

The men and boys of the community would congregate near the rifle range and coconut shies, showing off their skills and strength, with hitting the hammer. A prize would be forced upon them, china ornaments, beautiful colourful large soft toys would be in their arms as they walked away after spending their money, happy and contented as they moved from stall to stall.

There were shows there, one would enter, to see the snake charmer, or 'The Fattest Lady in the Land', or 'The Strongest Man', perhaps a freak of some loving animal which children would be most interested to see, but their parents usually advised against it.

Also the great big attraction was 'The Wall of Death'. A very high wooden building like the shape of a mill used for the grinding of corn, which would be vibrating from the inside activities, where the daring young motor bike riders were going round and round inside the building, faster, faster, climbing on the walls, then back to the ground.

Families of people would go round the Fair, children in pushchairs being pushed on the rough turf, while carrying a balloon in their hands. Young people running in and out of the stalls, chasing each other, wearing small paper hats they had bought for sixpence, with slogans on the front of them, such as were in fashion in the cinemas at the time. Confetti was thrown down people's necks and the youngsters used to split up into groups and go their own way by the end of the evening.

As it became darker, so the Fair would be lit up like fairyland, and the music sounded so gay, with the sound of laughter and voices wafting over the hill, till at last the big crowds dwindled away from the hill to make their way home, tired but happy and contented after such an exciting day. Open top buses would be quite frequent, but with so many people embarking on them, it very often meant many people walking all the way home, yet still hoping for the next Bank Holiday to come soon.

At last the Bank Holiday was at an end and the Fair packed up and moved off early the next day, to set up again in another place, leaving Portsdown Hill looking so bare and lonely with only the Forts at the top to guard it.

THE
Village Roadman

He was a quiet type of person going about his business, but he was very well liked and everyone knew him as 'the Roadman'. He would walk the roads in turn in our village, day in and day out, usually pushing an old grey cart, which contained the tools of his trade. These were a rather large hard broom, and a shovel, also a riphook and stone covered by a sack. The sack was his only cover for himself if the weather would come to rain. Then he would take shelter in a nearby hedge or ditch, usually he would be accompanied by a faithful companion, his little terrier dog, who did his share of work as well by chasing and killing any vermin which they might come across.

The job of the Roadman was to keep the paths and hedges trimmed, and fill any potholes in on the road, and of course cleaning out ditches and drains to enable the water to flow away, although there weren't any sewer drains in the village in those days, only rainwater drains which usually ended up in a pond. A few ponds were scattered about the village at a distance of about a mile away from each other. I remember as a child during the long summer holidays from school, how he would be cleaning out a ditch down the road where I lived. My childhood friends would all be standing nearby, watching, waiting, to see him throw a ball out of the ditch, one that had been considered lost for many days. Balls were in great demand and one only had a ball given them as a present at Christmas or birthdays, so losing one meant going without and no more ball games till another ball was acquired. In those days recreation areas were not in vogue in the village, so children usually played in the roads outside their homes or in fields nearby. The boys would aim at throwing a ball high over the roofs of buildings, thus many a ball would land in the guttering of the roof and would roll down when the rain was heavy, and so through playing in the roads the balls would also land in a ditch or hedge. Somehow the ditches were quite clean to what they are today, and one could often see the stones of many colours at the bottom with the water flowing gently over them. Many a time as children out on a long walk in the countryside, we would stop and cup our hands together and drink from a ditch, the water was clean and no harm came of it. The ponds were dirtier though, as horses would drink from them and very often would be washed down in the pond by the workman.

In the wider streams running under the road through the fields watercress would grow, and usually the streams were filled with small creatures, such as minnows and stickle-backs. Children would spend hours fishing for them with jam jars. As a stream passed under a road, on each side of the road an iron bar would be placed.

Always painted white it could be recognised from a distance away, so children found it easy to climb down into the stream, often falling in the water. During August each year, the Council would tar and gravel the roads while the weather was very hot.

It usually meant that our Roadman would also give a helping hand and work with the gang of men, and also a horse and cart would be hired from a farmer to carry the gravel. I remember before we had kerbstones along the road, how the sides of the road where there is a pavement now, would be very rough, so the Roadman would cut turf out from the banks and build up the pathway, keeping it a bit higher than the road which kept the pathway dryer for people to walk on. Sometimes his barrow would contain gravel and then he would fill up any holes in the road and also if the pathway became very muddy so a little gravel would be scattered over the pathway.

Thus the pavement would be started and with the coming of more people and traffic to the village so the roads were improved upon.

Our Roadman must have had a mine of information stored in his head, because he would often be stopped by passers-by inquiring about the whereabouts of certain places and persons in the village. It was always to the Roadman strangers would inquire. I can see him now,

Brooklyn Terrace with its made-up kerbed pavement

straightening up his body from his work, taking out his tobacco pouch and matches and pipe from his coat pocket. He would proceed to fill his pipe pressing in the tobacco well into the bowl, then with a few puffs after lighting it and with great thought puff more on his pipe. In the meanwhile in great thought of the question, he would then remove his pipe from his mouth. Then with great accuracy, he would explain the whereabouts of a certain person's home or how to arrive at a certain destination, and as one went on their way so he would stand and stare ahead of him thinking perhaps of other people and places he had known in his life.

Being a Roadman he was able to converse with great interest on the wildlife, and happenings in the village throughout the years. The villagers still remember him as he was, but alas there came the time when progress with modern machinery took over, and our very own Roadman faded from the village scene.

The hedgerows, banks and ditches, always so clean and tidy are now overgrown with weeds, tins and plastic bags and bottles, and make a sad picture wherever one walks through the villages today. Time doesn't stand still, and so with progress we enter into the future remembering 'the olden days' when man would do the work that machinery has now taken over.

'GREYLANDS'
During the War

Bessie (aged 17) when she worked at Barrowdene, Portsdown Hill
for a solicitor and his wife

It was in 1939 that I came to work at Greylands in Mill Road. It had been quite a year for me. To begin with I was at work on top of Portsdown Hill at a house called Barrowdene, working for a solicitor and his wife. I had a bad bout of 'flu, and then when I got better, it was somewhere in May of that year when I had the misfortune of breaking my leg which of course meant ten weeks at home which pleased me very much. I had been doing housework since I left school at 14 years and I hadn't been able to be at home very much as my jobs amounted to 'sleeping in'.

So home I came. Not long afterwards I had broken my leg and was walking all right again, I developed the mumps. What a painful complaint! Imagine at 18 years old having mumps so of course not being able to stay at my employment, so home I came once more, to Brooklyn Terrace in Anmore Road in Denmead. My nephew living with us at the time and only a baby also had mumps so I had plenty of interest to occupy me, but it was very irksome having to stay indoors and upstairs.

I was very glad to be back in Denmead, though as the War was imminent and being up on Portsdown Hill I seemed very much in the front line as it were, and I was pleased to think I'd feel safer in Denmead at home in familiar surroundings. Denmead was only ten miles from Portsmouth and it being a Naval town made things a bit worrying in the event of War and air raids.

We already had had practice sirens going for air raid alert and many shelters were built in the roads and gardens down the town, but somehow we never did get a shelter at Brooklyn Terrace. Our places of safety in an air raid would be the cupboard under the stairs or under the wooden table in the living room.

It was while I was at home with mumps that War was declared. I remember the radio on downstairs one morning and my mother calling up the stairs to me to tell me. Earlier I imagined if there was going to be a War I would somehow go up in an aeroplane and fly away to goodness knows where, but mumps stopped all that, so I came down to earth and realised I would be needed here in England to do my 'bit' as others were, although I was only between 17 and 18 years old.

It was while I was upstairs with mumps that I saw each day many barrage balloons rising to a good height in the sky over Portsdown Hill; each day there seemed to be a few more on the horizon never moving. They were erected on wires to protect the town and docks from enemy aircraft. It was very exciting to know things were happening around us. Many of my neighbours and friends were called up to serve the Country in different ways.

A few doors from our house lived two young ladies a little older than myself who had already enlisted into the Territorials down in Portsmouth. They had to leave home and go anywhere where the Army needed them, so they were on a 24-hour alert ready for War service, not knowing of what the future held for them. Each day someone in the village received their 'call-up' papers.

I found it was most interesting having to stay upstairs with mumps as I could go from the front to the back of the house, thus seeing things going on around me. Many housewives and the elderly men would volunteer for fire-watching and to be Air Raid Wardens where they might receive an arm band or a tin helmet. Each night one would hear voices in the road and would thankfully think how lucky they were, that someone would let them know if any danger from an air raid was imminent.

It was whilst I was recuperating that I was talking to a young man named Percy Lunn I used to go to school with, he was a little younger than myself and working up at the village shop 'Restall's' at the time.

Well, we had a discussion about how long the War would be on and I remember, and so does he to this day that I said, "If the War lasts I reckon it would probably go on for about ten years". He thought it would only last a very little while and the only thing I hoped was that I would live through it and afterwards be able to tell my grandchildren what their grandmother did during the War.

Well, I did live through it, but as regards telling grandchildren, well it wasn't to be as I never married till 1964 so hence no children.

I met up with him again when he came out of the Air Force and I was back home after serving in the WRAC, and he reminded me of that day, although he had enlisted in the Air Force and travelled to a good many places.

I still look back on the day when I was free from my mumps and able to start work again. I had left my previous job so I was able to take a job of work at Greylands as a general maid in domestic work, the kind of job I had been doing since I was 14 years old.

I still look back on that first day I started at Greylands. I remember walking down Mill Road and arriving at the 'House'. There was a large garden in front with a hedge very well cut, inside iron fencing with a fir tree hedge going down the side drive, leading to the back of the house. I wasn't sure, looking at the 'House', whether to pluck up courage and go to the front door or go round the back. I was saved from making a decision by the small dog of the house, a rather fattish type of terrier with a stubby tail and black spots. Later I learned his name was 'Spot'. Well, he came bounding up to me and barking quite loudly, while a lady was trying to keep up with him. She was rather a stately-looking lady dressed in a very dark dress, of course she recognised me at once and introduced herself as Nurse Firmin. She took my case from me and I followed her

Greylands, Mill Road

through round to the back of the house, up the steps to the kitchen door, where Miss Dugan was busy cooking a dish of a very tasty smell. Later I had my first meal at Greylands which was jugged hare with redcurrant sauce. I had never tasted such a dish before, so it's a meal I've never forgotten. Well my first sight then inside the kitchen was a table of plain wood scrubbed perfectly clean, not a mark on it. I thought, will I be able to keep up the standard or will it be too much? I was made so very welcome and learnt plenty in the ways of keeping and cleaning the house. It was very hard at times but being young, I was quite strong and healthy and nothing was too much. I used to take the dog out for a walk most days and also run messages to the village, so I got some amount of freedom, and then I would be able to call at home just to see my mother. I had to work from six o'clock in the morning and was expected to go to bed about 9.30 p.m.! I had one half day off a week from 2 p.m. if by then I had finished the cleaning up of the kitchen after the lunch. Sometimes I wouldn't be able to leave for my half day until 3 p.m.

*Mr Dugan, Miss Ruby Dugan, Nurse Firmin and a friend
(the family at Greylands)*

I also had every other Sunday off, mainly to be able to go to church in the evening.

Later on a canteen started up in the Church Hut run by the Vicar for the troops who were stationed in the village, so I was asked if I would like to help two evenings a week as Miss Dugan was able to let me go if I would care to. So of course I was pleased to accept as it meant having extra time off and was so very enjoyable although it meant being on my feet and serving up meals and washing up late into the evening but it was for a good cause.

A gardener was employed at Greylands, also a lady coming from Portsmouth once a week to do the washing. Sometimes she would bring her young grandson with her, but as the War was developing and she was in ill health she stopped coming and so I took on the washing.

The washing of the clothes was done out of doors down the garden under a creeper-covered sheltered roof. An old iron copper was used first filled with buckets of water from a tap in the garden and soda would be put in with a small amount of soap powder. The fire under the copper would be lit, burning any old wood, paper and rubbish. Sometimes if it was raining the clothes would hang up under the shelter to dry. It usually took an hour or more to get the water hot and to boiling point.

Wash house at Greylands

The garden at the back of the house was very pleasant to spend an hour or so in. It was wide and long and the pathways were set to be able to walk around the beds for flowers and rockeries. On each side of the garden grew lovely flowering trees and shrubs and the beds in the centre were mainly of roses, but the rockeries caught my attention more as they were always full of bloom for each season. Down towards the centre of the garden was a small pond with water lilies growing in it and a bridge over the pond gave it added attraction, round the sides grew iris and flowers and at one end the goldfish would come to the edge where the water was shallow.

Further on down the garden past the pond a greenhouse stood, then came the tennis court where many a tennis party was held. A large summer house was there and very often tea would be taken by me down to the court which meant a long way to carry trays and serve the people with a hot cup of tea and cakes. After the tennis court, came the orchard. I remember sides of the pathway leading down to the orchard used to be covered in primroses of different shades of yellow and pink pollinated by the bees.

I found much to do, although my work in the house was very pleasant and enjoyable. The house never got dirty; I think it was the lawn in front keeping the dust from the road, and there was never much traffic going by, like in the world of today.

One of my tasks was to scrub the front porch which consisted of tiles with stone steps leading on to it from the pathway. I remember on a frosty morning how the ice used to form on the tiles while I was trying to scrub them, how the wind used to blow the leaves back into the porch after I had swept them all away, and how my hands and arms used to be chapped owing to the wet and cold and how my knees would hurt through kneeling on the stone floor.

In the garden at the front of the house stood some bird baths of stone. It was a pleasure to watch the birds having their daily baths. So of course the baths would have to be scrubbed out and filled with clean water each day. I would also supply some cut up bread on the lawn. Sometimes 'Spot' the dog would run out of the house if he knew I was there and eat up all the bread.

Underneath the house was a big cellar, the windows being near to the ground were covered with glass and wire and usually stayed very dirty with overgrown shrubs.

Many a bird would get trapped between the wire and window and lose their lives. When one went down inside to the cellar one would have a very eerie feeling seeing dead birds and big spiders and horrible big slugs as sometimes the cellar would be very damp. Even the floor would contain quite a lot of water. The water at certain times of the year would rise up to three or four steps high, about three feet deep I have known it. Then to enable one to go down to the cellar we would need to walk on planks of wood.

The food would be kept up off the floor on a very large slatted table and also barrels of beer and bottles of wine would be standing on the floor.

Many a time I would have to tap a barrel and bring up glasses of beer. Whenever the gardener came he was always given a glass for his break time, also when a tradesman called, a glass of beer would be given him.

I certainly turned against beer although I had never tasted it, seeing it in wooden barrels, and especially as there were many little flies always buzzing around where the taps were, as a dish would be under the tap to catch any drips.

When the air raids were on we sometimes used to sleep down in the cellar as it was supposed to be a safe place if a bomb should fall. Very often we would stay in our beds upstairs and hope for the best.

We had some very bad air raids in Denmead, as Portsmouth was only ten miles away and many enemy aircraft would fly over the country, unload their bombs and fly back to Germany.

I remember on one occasion being down the garden one afternoon, about 3.45 p.m. when the children were coming out of school, when a low-flying aircraft came over with his guns firing. So I ran back towards the house and tried to get back into the kitchen, but when I arrived up the steps to the back door the door wouldn't open owing to the vibration of the aeroplane. Mr Dugan managed to come to the door and between us it opened and being well frightened I was glad to be indoors and safe. Later on, venturing to go outdoors gain, there on the step was a bullet. I think Mr Dugan kept it!

There were many air raids at that time and a great thing Mr Dugan did for our safety in the house was to have fixed on the floor below each window great lengths of thick rope to enable, in the event of fire, to throw the rope out of the window and climb down. We never had to, as it never happened, thanks to our team of fire watchers and warden in Mill Road. There were many incendiary bombs dropping around us and many land mines which usually ended up in trees, as I think a parachute would have been attached to the mines. They did quite a bit of damage to houses on the Hambledon Road towards Waterlooville. I worked as a voluntary fire watcher, and also a canteen worker for the troops at the Church Hut, so my spare time, although still working full-time for Miss Dugan, was taken up with these duties. When fire watching two of us would be on duty all night once a week. We still had to carry out our ordinary jobs the next day, but in any case if there was a raid we would be awake, so many people would sleep in the daytime if they were able.

All Saints' Church - Nurse Firmin and dog 'Spot' at the gate
and the Church Hut in the background

At Greylands a rather large building stood at the back, known as the Billiard Room. Many Officers and local gentlemen would be invited by Mr Dugan of an evening to enjoy a game of billiards. A man in the village was employed especially to take care of the table. I remember seeing him iron the baize and I remember the low large green lampshades overhanging the table. I used to take in refreshments which to me, being in my teens was quite an experience in its own way.

It was while I was working for Miss Dugan that two little girls of school age came to stay. They had been previously evacuated to 'Wolverton' in Anmore Road, but the lady who owned the house being rather elderly found them too much to look after, so Miss Dugan took on the job of housing them, especially as I was able to help, but after a few months Miss Dugan decided to let their mother have them back, so as to be evacuated to Leicester to stay with their grandmother. Not long after (such a sad affair) the children and their grandmother were in an air raid and all lost their lives through enemy action. It took a great deal of understanding of the unfortunate accident that I couldn't wait to join the ATS and do my bit. I had just lost one brother killed in the Navy, and another brother was in Malta in the Hampshire Regiment. He was buried alive for eight hours but I am pleased to say he came through the War all right, so it was tragedies like these happening that brought the War closer to Denmead. Many of our neighbours had lost someone and many tragedies occurred.

Miss Dugan was very kind to people and if anyone was in distress or ill she would always try and comfort them, such as visiting the families and taking food to them such as a bowl of soup or some other kind of nourishment for the sick and dying; also Nurse who was at Greylands would go each afternoon when off duty to visit and talk to the elderly, which was always greatly appreciated.

It was a sad day when Nurse Firmin herself developed an illness and had to go away to hospital.

I stayed for three years at Greylands. It was my home while I worked there. Sad and very happy years to look back on. My memories of the house and garden were very pleasant as many years after I would visit Miss Dugan, and always we would walk down through the garden while Miss Dugan would cut a rose off each bush for me to take home a bunch of beautiful roses for my mother.

I remember outside the kitchen window at Greylands grew a lovely rose, Albertine, covering the trellis, so beautiful with a lovely perfume.

By the trellis gate on the side of the driveway would grow trees of different coloured broom and leading into the garden near the billiard room stood the pergola which was covered with red roses and honeysuckle and a walled garden which contained various coloured spirea. The parrot, a green Amazon, would spend many hours on the pergola without thinking of flying away. The parrot was a good talker and was kept in the lounge usually on a stand and in a cage, but he died while I was there and Miss Dugan eventually had another one the same kind from a friend at Botley, which was just as tame.

Although a gardener was employed I would spend many hours with Miss Dugan working on the rockeries weeding them mostly, and 'Spot' the dog played his part too, as when the pond needed cleaning out, as the weed used to grow very quickly, he would stand by waiting to catch a grass snake of about three feet in length which usually during the summer would be in the pond. 'Spot' would get hold of it and shake it till it died, then 'Spot' would be very sick, but being a terrier he loved the sport of it.

He used to like running behind me while I rode my bicycle up and back to the shops; it was quite safe in those days as the only vehicles on the road would be military or the doctor's car so mostly the roads would be deserted except for people walking. Yes, he was a good companion, and I was sorry to leave Greylands, but in August 1942 I had my papers come for me to join up in the ATS, but every leave I came home I would always be invited to call on Miss Dugan. I kept in touch with her till she moved out of the village and took a place on her own at West Meon.

(M)HAA Reg. 584, 1942

After the War

*After the War Bessie worked in horticulture,
at Tayler's Nursery, Denmead*

*WRAC TA Band (Portsmouth) - 583 Regiment, 1950's
Bessie the drummer girl*

EPILOGUE
Hampshire

Do I know Hampshire? Although living here for the best part of my life I still find there are many places which I've never seen except by looking at a map.

I often wonder why I have no ambition to live elsewhere in the world. Of course, having been born and bred in Hampshire, still living in the same home and village I was born in, and being of Hampshire ancestors, it's only natural that I remain.

Bessie drove TA trucks throughout England and Wales, 1950's

Until the War of 1939 came I hadn't travelled very far afield. London was about as far as I had been. I was called up in the Services and found I had to leave home. I served on gun sites in different parts of England and Wales, then eventually I drove trucks around the countryside for the Territorial Army. Well, in those days to find one's way about one had to use a map as all names of places and roads were obliterated.

I happened to be posted to the Militia Camp at Botley, I really felt as though I had come back home. At least I was only in cycling distance of Denmead, so I no longer felt homesick. I had been in the ATS a few years then, and mingled with people and service personnel from many parts of the globe.

I was often named a 'Hampshire Hog', though for which purpose such a name was thought up, I never knew. I was so proud of my County and I still am to this day.

We have everything to enable us to enjoy life, such as good living off the land and social activities of all descriptions from horse riding, walking, sailing, flying or swimming.

The history of Hampshire often meets up with one as we travel the roads to see the beautiful New Forest. The famous ports of Southampton and Portsmouth had many ships built with oak trees from the Forest, the most famous probably being the 'Mary Rose'.

The small flintstone cottages with thatched roofs, the flints being quarried from the fields nearby. What a sight meets one while travelling along a motorway! The wide expanse of land with acres of golden corn growing and luscious green meadows with animals grazing in contentment. Come off the motorway and travel on the narrow lanes with twists and turns and small narrow bridges to see masses of celandines along the banks where the water trickles along the ditches by the side of the road. Eventually travelling along to see a large wood with beautiful green beech trees growing in a carpet of thousands of bluebells, a sight never to be forgotten.

There are small hamlets or villages with most curious names; I often wonder how such names of villages were arrived at. I suppose there is a story attached to each place.

The County has so much of interest to offer: such beautiful views, the green hedgerows guarding the plots of land round each cottage. Homes of every variety and the different types of buildings which have been erected for hundreds of years. Now and again a church or castle or abbey, some so old they are crumbling.

Also in the towns one can still meet the old and the new, side by side, each playing a part in the modern world. But what I feel makes Hampshire so attractive are the people who each live separate lives yet are always there when one needs them. Their ways may be old fashioned compared to a Londoner for example, but they are staunch and true and have great beliefs in the right ways of doing things in life. Often slow in talking, but with good humour, interest, and honesty they make their way in life and always for the benefit of mankind of any nationality.

Yes, could you visit Hampshire and then forget it?

I don't think so.

Bessie and Jessie Card visiting Greylands in recent times - Jessie worked at Greylands before Bessie